Jordan's Catch

Story by Stephen Harrison
Illustrations by Al Fiorentino

NELSON PRICE MILBURN

All the children stood and watched
as the ball flew off the bat
and went high in the air.
"It's coming to you, Jordan," called Kris.
"It's your catch!"

Jordan looked up
and ran towards the ball.
He watched the ball coming down.
He held up his hands to catch it
as it dropped out of the sky.

The ball hit Jordan's hands and bounced up. He grabbed at it, but it slipped through his fingers. He lost his balance and fell over.

Jordan lay on the grass
and watched the ball
rolling towards the fence.
"I'm sorry," he said to Kris.
"I lost the game for us."

"Oh, don't worry," said Kris.
"Everyone drops catches."

"Cheer up, Jordan," said Dad
as they went home.
"I've got a surprise for you.
Look—I've been given two tickets
for the big match tomorrow."

"Hey, that's great, Dad," said Jordan.
"Our home team is playing
for the cup!"

"I'll watch it later on television,"
said Mum.
"You go with Dad, Jordan,
and forget about dropping that catch.
I'm sure you'll take the next one
that comes to you."

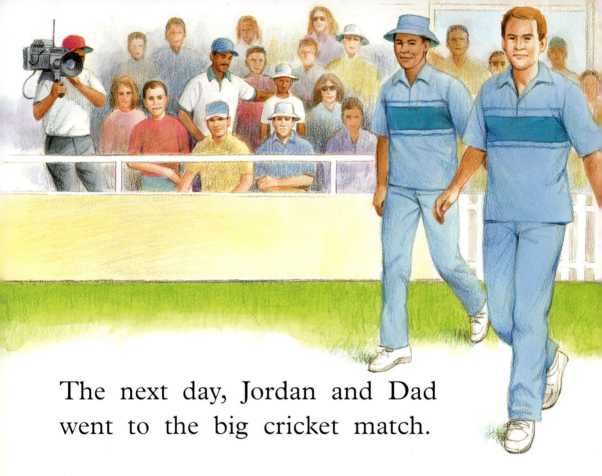

The next day, Jordan and Dad went to the big cricket match.

"Look at all the television cameras!" said Jordan as they sat down.

"There's one right by us," said Dad. "We might see ourselves on television later."

The players came onto the field,
and the game began.

The other team batted first,
and the runs came quickly.
Then the wickets started to fall.

Jordan and Dad shouted and cheered
with the rest of the crowd.

After lunch,
it was the home team's turn to bat,
and at first they scored well.
It was very exciting.
"We could win the cup!" said Jordan.

There was only one ball left,
and they still needed six runs to win.
The batsman had just **one** chance.
He stepped forward
and swung at the last ball of the match.
With a mighty hit
he sent it flying up into the air.

"It's a **six!**" yelled Jordan.

The crowd roared
as the ball flew high over the boundary.

"Look, Dad!" cried Jordan.
"The ball is coming this way!"
The man in front of them stood up
and tried to catch the ball
as it came towards them.
But he could only just touch it
with his fingertips.

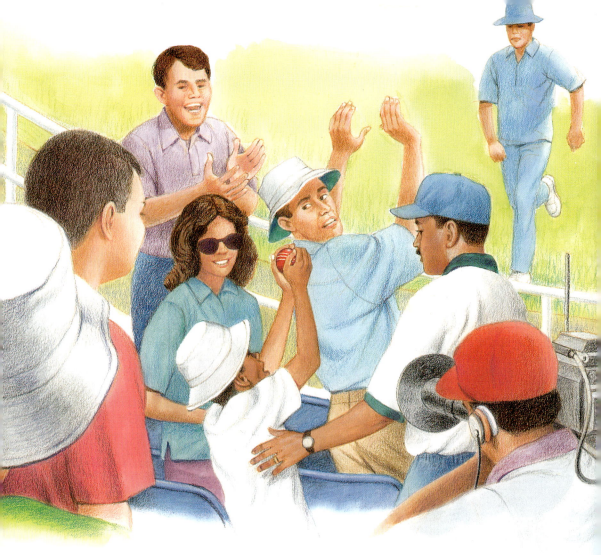

The ball fell down and,
without thinking,
Jordan reached out and caught it.
Everyone clapped and cheered.

When they got home,
Mum was just turning the television on.
"We'll watch the highlights with you,"
said Dad, smiling at Jordan.

"What a good hit!" said Mum,
as they watched the last ball
flying up into the air.

Then Mum sat forward and stared
at the television in surprise.

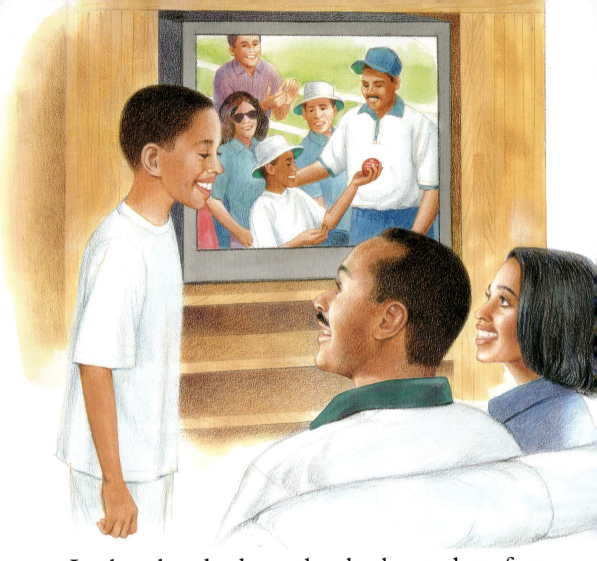

Jordan laughed at the look on her face. "You were right, Mum," he said. "I **did** take the next catch that came to me!"